Birthday Cakes

Birthday Cakes

Easy to make and spectacular to look at!

Love Food ® is an imprint of Parragon Books Ltd

Parragon
Queen Street House
4 Queen Street
Bath BA1 1HE, UK

Copyright © Parragon Books Ltd 2007

Love Food ® and the accompanying heart device is a trademark of Parragon Books Ltd.

ISBN 978-1-4054-9579-0

Printed in China

Produced by the Buenavista Studio s.l.
Text and Recipes by Oliver Trific
Edited by Fiona Biggs
Photography by Günter Beer
Home Economy by Stevan Paul
Design by Cammaert & Eberhardt

Notes for the reader

This book uses imperial, metric, and US cup measurements. Follow the same units of measurement
throughout; do not mix imperial and metric. All spoon measurements are level: teaspoons are assumed
to be 5 ml, and tablespoons are assumed to be 15 ml. Unless otherwise stated, milk is assumed to be
whole, and eggs and fruit such as bananas are medium. Recipes using raw or very lightly cooked eggs
should not be served to infants, the elderly, pregnant women, convalescents, and anyone suffering from
an illness. The times given are approximate only.

Contents

 # Basic Recipes

Birthday cakes naturally need to taste as good as they look. Moist cake and creamy frosting are the delicious canvas for the whimsical creations in this book. The following recipes are simple, quick, and taste just great.

Chocolate Cake

½ cup unsalted butter, melted, plus extra for greasing

1¾ cups granulated sugar

2 large eggs

¾ cup unsweetened cocoa

1¾ cups all-purpose flour, plus extra, for dusting

1½ tsp baking powder

1½ tsp baking soda

1 tsp salt

1 cup milk (or ½ cup milk and ½ cup sour cream)

2 tsp vanilla extract

1 cup boiling water

Everyone loves a chocolate cake. The scent of chocolate is difficult to resist, even more so if the cake is covered with rich, creamy frosting.

Makes 1 large cake or 2 small cakes

Bring the refrigerated ingredients to room temperature. Preheat the oven to 350°F/175°C. Grease a 10 x 12-inch/25 x 30-cm rectangular cake pan or two 8–9-inch/20–23-cm round cake pans, line with parchment paper, and grease and flour the paper. Dust the inside of the pan with flour and tap out the excess.

Using an electric mixer, cream the butter and sugar until smooth and light in color. Beat in one egg at a time, ensuring that each is completely incorporated into the batter before adding the next.

Sift the cocoa, flour, baking powder, baking soda, and salt into a separate bowl. Add the cocoa mixture to the mixing bowl alternately with the milk, then add the vanilla and beat on medium speed for 2 minutes. Add the boiling water and beat to combine well (the mixture will be on the thin side). Pour into the prepared pan.

Place the pan in the center of the oven and bake for 30–35 minutes or until a skewer inserted in the center of the cake comes out clean. Remove from the oven and let cool in the pan on a cooling rack. After 10 minutes, loosen the cake from the sides of the pan with a butter knife or spatula, shake the pan to make sure the cake is not sticking to it, and invert onto a cooling rack. Let cool completely before frosting.

Banana Cake

unsalted butter, for greasing

2 cups all-purpose flour, plus extra for dusting

1 tsp baking powder

¾ tsp baking soda

½ tsp salt

4 bananas

2 large eggs

1 cup granulated sugar

½ cup vegetable oil

1 tsp vanilla extract

½ cup buttermilk

Bananas turn a simple white cake into a moist sensation. Rich and delicious, this cake goes perfectly with any "exotic" frosting, such as Cream Cheese Coconut Frosting (see page 20).

Makes 1 large cake or 2 small cakes

Preheat the oven to 350°F/175°C. Grease a 10 x 12-inch/25 x 30-cm rectangular cake pan or two 8–9-inch/20–23-cm round cake pans, line with parchment paper, and grease and flour the paper. Dust the inside of the pan with flour and tap out the excess.

Sift the flour, baking soda, baking powder, and salt into a bowl and set aside. Peel the bananas and mash with a fork.

Using an electric mixer set at medium speed, beat the eggs and sugar until fluffy and light. Add the oil, then the vanilla extract, and mix well. Add the mashed bananas and continue beating until well blended.

Pour in the flour mixture and buttermilk alternately, starting and finishing with the flour mixture. Mix until just blended, then pour into the prepared pan.

Place the pan on the center rack of the oven and bake for 30 minutes or until a skewer comes out clean. Remove from the oven and let cool on a cooling rack. When cool, loosen the cake from the sides of the pan, invert, remove the parchment paper, and reinvert back onto the rack. Let cool completely before cutting into layers and frosting.

Sour Cream Pound Cake

1 cup unsalted butter, cut into small pieces, plus extra for greasing

3 cups all-purpose flour

½ tsp baking powder

¼ tsp baking soda

½ tsp salt

3 cups granulated sugar

6 large eggs

1 tsp vanilla extract

1 tsp lemon extract (or grated zest of 1 lemon, if preferred)

1 cup sour cream

Tangy sour cream adds a rich new flavor dimension to traditional pound cake. This is a perfect recipe for the adult cakes in this book.

Makes 1 cake

Preheat the oven to 325°F/160°C. Bring the refrigerated ingredients to room temperature. Grease a 10-inch/25-cm tube pan or Bundt pan, line with parchment paper, and grease and flour the paper. Dust the inside of the pan with flour and tap out the excess.

Sift the flour, baking powder, baking soda, and salt into a bowl. In a second bowl, using an electric mixer set at medium speed, beat the butter and sugar until fluffy and light, 3–4 minutes. Beat in one egg at a time, ensuring that each is completely incorporated into the batter before adding the next. Add the vanilla extract and lemon extract.

Add a third of the flour mixture to the butter mixture, add half of the sour cream, and beat. Continue to add the flour and the remaining sour cream, finishing with the final portion of flour. Scrape the sides of the mixing bowl once or twice with a rubber or silicone spatula to mix in all the batter.

Pour the batter into the pan and smooth it out evenly. Tap the underside of the pan repeatedly to release any air trapped in the batter. Place the pan in the oven and bake for 1 hour 15 minutes, or until a skewer comes out clean when inserted in the cake.

Remove the cake from the oven and let cool for at least 15 minutes on a cooling rack. Gently invert the cake onto a second rack, and let cool completely before frosting.

Cook's Tip: If you have more batter than your pan can hold, leave space at the top, pour the remaining batter into a second small cake pan, and bake separately.

Carrot Cake

unsalted butter or nonstick spray,
for greasing

2 cups all-purpose flour, plus
extra for dusting

1 cup walnut pieces

2 cups granulated sugar

2 tsp baking soda

1 tsp baking powder

1 tbsp ground cinnamon

½ tsp salt

3 large eggs, at room temperature

1 cup vegetable oil

2½ cups grated carrot

1 cup crushed pineapple,
well drained

Grated carrot and chopped walnuts make this cake a taste treat. Simply irresistible, it will turn even the most staunch carrot cake doubter into a believer. And, best of all, because it is made in a food processor, it is almost as quick to prepare as it is to eat!

Makes 1 cake

Preheat the oven to 350°F/175°C. Grease a 10-inch/25-cm springform pan, line with parchment paper, and grease and flour the paper. Dust the inside of the pan with flour and tap out the excess.

Process the walnuts in a food processor for several seconds, until chopped into small pieces, and set aside.

Using the blade attachment, combine all the dry ingredients in the food processor for 10 seconds. Add the eggs and the oil, and process for an additional 30 seconds. Remove and pour into a large mixing bowl.

Add the walnut pieces, grated carrot, and crushed pineapple to the mixture and stir until well blended—the batter will be very thick.

Pour the mixture into the prepared pan and place on the center rack of the oven. Bake for 60–70 minutes or until a skewer inserted in the center of the cake comes out clean.

Allow the cake to cool in the pan on a cooling rack for at least 15 minutes. With a narrow spatula or butter knife, gently separate the sides of the cake from the pan. Release the spring latch and remove the side of the pan. Place the rack over the cake top, flip over, and remove the pan bottom and the parchment paper. Allow to cool thoroughly before cutting.

Yogurt Sponge Cake

¾ cup unsalted butter, at room temperature, cut into small pieces, plus extra for greasing

2½ cups all-purpose flour, plus extra for dusting

1½ cups granulated sugar

3 large eggs

1 tsp baking powder

1 tsp baking soda

¾ tsp salt

1 cup plain yogurt

2 tsp vanilla extract

½ tsp almond extract

Moist, with just the right amount of sweetness, this cake is the perfect foundation for any type of frosting. But it is delicious on its own, as well!

Makes 1 large cake or 2 small cakes

Bring all the refrigerated ingredients to room temperature. Preheat the oven to 350°F/175°C. Grease a 10 x 12-inch/25 x 30-cm rectangular cake pan or two 8–9-inch/20–23-cm round cake pans, line with parchment paper, and grease and flour the paper. Dust the inside of the pan with flour and tap out the excess.

Using an electric mixer, cream the butter and sugar until smooth and light in color. Beat in one egg at a time, ensuring that each is completely incorporated into the batter before adding the next. Scrape the sides of the mixing bowl with a rubber or silicone spatula once or twice to mix in all the batter.

Sift the dry ingredients into a bowl and set aside. In another bowl, combine the yogurt, vanilla extract, and almond extract and whisk together.

Add the dry ingredients and the yogurt mixture alternately to the batter in the mixing bowl, ladling in large spoons of each, starting and finishing with the flour. Mix until just well blended. Pour into the prepared pan and place in the center of the preheated oven. Bake for 35 minutes or until a skewer inserted in the center of the cake comes out clean.

Remove from the oven and let cool on a cooling rack. Gently loosen the cake from the sides of the pan, and tap the pan a few times to make sure the cake separates from it. Invert onto the cooling rack and let cool completely. Frost when the cake is completely cooled.

Buttercream Frosting

Buttercream can be made in advance and stored, tightly covered, in a cool place, for up to 1 day. It may not be suitable when outdoor temperatures are very high, but a buttercream-frosted cake can be stored in the refrigerator until needed.

Makes enough to frost 1 cake

1 cup unsalted butter, at room temperature

5 cups confectioners' sugar, sifted

2–3 tbsp milk

1 tsp vanilla extract

For white frosting

Using an electric mixer with the paddle attachment or a handheld electric mixer with the egg beater attachment, beat the butter until light and fluffy. Sift the confectioners' sugar twice and add to the butter with the milk and vanilla. Fold in carefully, then beat until pale and creamy. Add more milk if necessary. The consistency should be marshmallow-like, easy to handle but not liquid. Color the buttercream with food coloring, if desired.

For chocolate frosting

Melt 4 ounces of good quality chocolate, let cool but not harden, and beat into the Buttercream Frosting, or dissolve 1 tablespoon of unsweetened cocoa in 1–2 tablespoons of hot water. Let cool and beat into the Buttercream Frosting. If adding melted chocolate or unsweetened cocoa, reduce the milk by half when making the basic frosting.

Dark Chocolate Frosting

Deep, dark chocolate flavor rolled into a buttery frosting, this is a dream frosting for chocolate lovers.

Makes enough to frost 1 cake

1 cup butter, softened

½–¾ cup unsweetened cocoa

2¾ cups confectioners' sugar

⅓ cup milk, plus extra, if needed

1 tsp vanilla extract

Using an electric mixer with the paddle attachment or a handheld electric mixer with the egg beater attachment, beat the butter until light and fluffy.

Sift together the cocoa and sugar and add to the butter, together with the milk and vanilla extract. Fold in carefully, then beat until creamy and spreadable. Add more milk in small amounts until the desired consistency is reached.

Refrigerate, covered, until ready to use.

Cream Cheese Coconut Frosting

Cream cheese frosting is a perennial favorite, and the shredded coconut gives this version a completely new twist. Try it on the Carrot Cake or the Banana Cake.

Makes enough to frost 1 cake

1 lb/450 g cream cheese, at room temperature

½ cup unsalted butter, at room temperature

1½ tsp vanilla extract

2½ cups confectioners' sugar, sifted

2 tbsp milk

½ cup shredded coconut

Using an electric mixer, beat the cream cheese, butter, and vanilla extract in a large bowl until smooth. Add the sugar a cup at a time, beating well. Stir in the milk and coconut, and mix. The frosting can be used immediately or refrigerated until ready to use.

Whipped Sour Cream Frosting

This is the perfect frosting when you are short on time. Prepare this frosting directly when needed and serve the cake as soon as possible, since the whipped cream does not hold up for long.

Makes enough to frost 1 cake

1 cup heavy cream

1 cup confectioners' sugar

1 cup sour cream or plain yogurt

Beat the cream while slowly adding the sugar. Continue to beat until soft peaks form. Remove from the mixer and fold in the sour cream. Refrigerate until ready to use.

Cook's Tip: When using as a filling between two cake layers, spread on the bottom layer to within 1 inch/2.5 cm of the edges, as the frosting is soft and will ooze out of the sides when the layers are pressed together.

Decorating Marzipan

Possibly of Persian origin, marzipan is a mixture of ground almonds and sugar, roasted together to create a deliciously sweet confection.

Makes enough to cover 1 cake

6 oz/175 g marzipan

3 oz/85 g confectioners' sugar, plus extra for dusting

food coloring, as desired

Mix the marzipan with the sugar and gently knead until smooth. Divide into smaller amounts and color, as desired, with food coloring. Knead thoroughly for solid color marzipan; combining less well will result in a streaky effect.

Dust the counter with sugar to prevent the marzipan from sticking to the surface. Be generous, as the marzipan will absorb a little of the sugar when worked. When the desired color has been achieved, stop working the marzipan, as it will become slightly crumbly if kneaded excessively.

When incorporating the sugar into the marzipan be sure not to knead too forcefully, as this will cause the marzipan to separate and become crumbly. Subsequently, too much kneading should also be avoided.

As a basic guideline use 2 parts marzipan to 1 part confectioners' sugar (for example 10 oz/280 g marzipan to 5 oz/140 g sugar). Adding more sugar will create a stiffer modeling marzipan, which can be helpful if you are creating figures with limbs, rose stems, etc.

Keep marzipan, covered, in a cool place, for up to 1 day.

Cook's Tip: It is best to wear latex gloves when working with marzipan and food coloring, to avoid getting your fingers dyed.

First Birthday Cakes

Baby's first birthday is always special. Add a personal touch to the moment with these heartwarming cakes. The following recipes will delight friends and relatives just as much as the birthday baby.

Alphabet Block Cake

1 quantity Yogurt Sponge Cake
(see page 16)

2 quantities Buttercream
Frosting—white (see page 18)

food coloring in desired colors,
to color frosting

Make baby's first birthday special with this delightful, easy-to-make cake. If you are short on time, you can use tubes of prepared colored icing to decorate the cake.

Bake the cake in a 9 x 9-inch/23 x 23-cm square cake pan. Let cool before frosting.

Color the frosting with different shades of food coloring. When adding colors to the frosting, start with only a few drops of food coloring and mix it into a small amount of frosting. Add more frosting or coloring until you reach the desired color.

Cut the cake horizontally into 2 layers of equal thickness. Frost the top of one of the layers, place the other cake on top, and frost the top and sides of the cake with one quantity of frosting.

Using a ruler or straight edge, divide the cake into 9 sections and make a small indentation with the ruler, as if you were creating a tic-tac-toe grid. This determines the outline of the blocks.

Color the remaining frosting as desired (with at least 3 colors) and transfer the frosting to separate piping bags equipped with small-holed tips. Outline a box within each box, about ¼ inch/5 mm in from the ruler indentations, alternating the colors as you decorate.

Decorate the numbers, letters, or designs into every box. Decorate the sides of the cake in the same way.

Cook's Tip: Decorate the cake freehand for a more childlike appearance.

Flying Balloons Cake

1 quantity Yogurt Sponge Cake
(see page 16)

1 quantity Buttercream
Frosting—white (see page 18)

1 quantity Decorating Marzipan
(see page 22)

food coloring, as needed

24-inch/60-cm black licorice
string

Brighten up any birthday party with this colorful cake. The balloons are simple to make and will definitely catch the eye of the birthday boy or girl.

Bake the batter in a 12-inch/30-cm round cake pan. Let cool completely before frosting.

When cooled, cut the cake in half horizontally. Frost the top of one half. Place the second half on top of the first and use the remaining frosting to frost the top layer evenly. Use a palette knife to create a very even surface.

Create 3–5 different-colored marzipan mixtures. Roll each into a cylinder and cut into discs. Leave the discs round, or shape them into ovals. Place the discs on the cake. Cut the licorice string into 2-inch/5-cm lengths and place them on the cake to create the balloon strings. Vary the lengths if desired.

Cook's Tip: You can make a long marzipan ribbon to wrap around the cake by preparing the basic marzipan recipe for decorating and rolling it thin on a floured counter. Using a pizza wheel, cut the marzipan into strips. Place them around the cake for the ribbon, connecting the ends as necessary.

Puppy Dog Cake

1 quantity Yogurt Sponge Cake
(see page 16)

1 quantity Buttercream
Frosting—white (see page 18)

½ quantity Decorating Marzipan
(see page 22)

pink and green food coloring

confectioners' sugar, for dusting

licorice string

junior mints

Every child wants a puppy dog. You can help make that dream come true, with this charming cake.

Bake the batter in two 9-inch/23-cm round cake pans. Reserve some batter to make 2 standard cupcakes. Let cool completely before frosting.

Frost the top of one cake. Place the second cake on top and use the remaining frosting to frost the cake and the two cupcakes evenly.

Color two thirds of the decorating marzipan with the pink food coloring, and color the remainder with the green. Roll out the pink marzipan on a surface dusted with confectioners' sugar, cut into a long thin strip, and wrap this around the large cake to make the dog's leash. Knead together the remainder and form the dog's tongue.

Cut out two small discs of green marzipan for the eyes. Place the tongue and eyes on the cake as indicated in the photo on page 31. Use the licorice string to outline the ears and jowls. Cut one piece of licorice in half and place one half on each eye. Place 3 mints on each cupcake paw, and one mint above the tongue to form the nose. Scatter the remaining mints randomly over the cake to create the dog's spots.

Centipede or Inchworm Cake

1 quantity Yogurt Sponge Cake
(see page 16)

1 quantity Buttercream
Frosting—white (see page 18)

assorted food coloring

two-toned marshmallows

some licorice string

jelly fruits

jelly candies

Perfect for any birthday, this delightful idea is a great cake for the busy parent. Just bake the cupcakes a day or two in advance and store them in an airtight container until needed, then make 2 short centipedes or 1 long centipede.

Divide the batter among 12 paper cupcake cups that have been placed in a standard 12-cup muffin pan. Bake for 15–20 minutes. Let the cupcakes cool in the pan for 10 minutes, then invert onto a cooling rack and cool completely.

Divide the frosting into equal portions and color each portion as you wish. Generously cover the top of each cupcake with frosting.

Decorate one cupcake as the face, using sliced marshmallows for the eyes, licorice string for the mouth and eyebrows, and a fruit gum for the nose. Decorate the remaining cupcakes as you like. You can use candy to decorate the feet for a centipede, or omit them to create an inchworm.

Teddy Bear Cake

2 quantities Yogurt Sponge Cake (see page 16)

unsalted butter, for greasing

all-purpose flour, for dusting

1 quantity Buttercream Frosting—white (see page 18)

brown and yellow food coloring

1 quantity Decorating Marzipan (see page 22)

two-toned jelly candies

This friendly bear will delight the youngest guests at any birthday party. You can also use real hats, ribbons, or bows to decorate it.

Prepare a 10-inch/25-cm springform cake pan and 3 paper cupcake cups. Grease the cake pan, line with parchment paper, and grease and flour the paper. Dust the inside of the pan with flour and tap out the excess. Divide the batter among the prepared pan and paper cups and bake, reducing the baking time to approximately 15–20 minutes for the cupcakes.

Cool the cakes in the pan and paper cases for 15 minutes. Invert the cakes onto cooling racks and let cool for one hour, or until completely cooled.

In a small bowl, dye the frosting with brown and yellow colorings to make the desired brown color for the bear; blend well.

Frost the large cake and place with the flat end down on a serving platter. Frost the small cakes, placing one each at the top of the head to form the bear's ears and one in the middle of the cake to form the snout.

Cut some marzipan into thin strips and reserve. Dye the remaining marzipan brown, and shape the eyes, eyebrows, nose, and mouth of the bear. Place on the cake. Place the reserved marzipan strips on the eyes. Use jelly candies to form a bow on top of the bear's head, as well as a collar at the bottom of the head.

Smiling Fish Cake

1 quantity Yogurt Sponge Cake (see page 16)

1 quantity Cream Cheese Coconut Frosting (see page 20)

1 quantity Decorating Marzipan (see page 22)

blue food coloring

This cake will definitely make an impression, perfect if your toddler is a fan of all things aquatic!

Bake the batter in two 8-inch/20-cm round cake pans. Let cool completely before frosting.

When cooled, frost the top of one of the cakes. Place the second cake on top and use the remaining frosting to frost the cake evenly. Use a palette knife to create a wavy surface. If you like, you can omit the coconut from the frosting.

Make 2 equal-sized balls and 3 little triangular teeth out of uncolored marzipan. Dye the remaining marzipan with blue food coloring. Make 2 discs, 2 dorsal fins, and a large tail fin by modeling the marzipan into the required shapes. Roll two pieces of marzipan into thin cords of varying lengths to form the lips. Place the marzipan pieces on the frosted cake, as seen on page 37.

Candy Store Cake

1 quantity Carrot Cake
(see page 14)

1 quantity Cream Cheese Coconut
Frosting (see page 20)

red food coloring, as needed

any assorted candies such as

    licorice pieces

    chocolate drops

    mini-marshmallows

    jellybeans

    sugar-coated almonds

This cake is fun and versatile; there is no limit to what kind of candy you can add. Select your favorites and get decorating.

Bake the cake in two 8-inch/20-cm round cake pans, and let cool before frosting and decorating.

Add a few drops of red food coloring until a bright pink color is achieved. Cover the top of one cake layer with frosting, place the second layer on top, and frost the top and sides of the cake. Swirl the frosting to create a wavy look. Refrigerate the cake until needed.

Shortly before serving, remove the cake from the refrigerator. Scatter candies over the entire cake, according to taste. Do not place the cake in the refrigerator once the candies are on the cake as they will draw moisture and their coloring will begin to bleed into the frosting.

Kids' Birthday Cakes

As they get a little older, kids will appreciate more extravagant birthday cake designs. Try the following recipes and make their big day extra special with cakes that look and taste spectacular.

Dinosaur Cake

1 quantity Sour Cream Pound
Cake (see page 12)

5 oz/140 g semisweet chocolate
pieces

6 tbsp vegetable shortening

3 quantities Decorating Marzipan
(see page 22)

pink food coloring (or any shade
you desire)

Just the ticket for the dino-crazy kid in your home. Use artificial trees and other gear from model suppliers to create an authentic Jurassic age feeling on the table.

Bake the cake in a heart-shaped pan measuring approximately 13 x 12 inches/ 33 x 30 cm. Let cool.

Melt the chocolate and vegetable shortening in a double boiler, or put the chocolate pieces in a metal bowl and place over a pan of simmering water. The chocolate will melt slowly, so leave it alone (no need to stir) and watch it carefully. Stir to blend the chocolate and shortening, keeping the glaze warm in the double boiler.

Cut the cake in half, and then sandwich the halves together using some glaze to bond them. Place the cake on a cooling rack with the rounded side up.

Divide 1 quantity of the marzipan in half. Set half aside.

Shape one third of the remaining marzipan into a tail and attach it to the lowest end of the cake. Mold one third into a head-like shape and place it on the other end of the cake. Shape the final third into spikes and a cord the length of the top seam of the cake. Lay the cord over the seam and stud with the marzipan spikes.

Pour the remaining glaze over the cake and let cool. Carefully transfer the cake to a serving platter, using a large palette knife to support the entire length of the cake.

Dye half of the remaining marzipan. Mold 4 feet, 2 eyes, and a snout out of the colored marzipan. Mold the remainder into claws, eyebrows, and eyeballs. Place these on and around the cake, as shown on page 43.

Castle Cake

1 quantity Yogurt Sponge Cake
(see page 16)

1 quantity Buttercream
Frosting—white (see page 18)

yellow food coloring

jelly fruits or gumdrops

1 graham cracker square or other
square cookie

licorice string

1½ quantities Decorating
Marzipan
(see page 22)

red food coloring

orange food coloring

green food coloring

Is your kid crazy for knights and all things medieval? Why not make it a birthday to remember with this authentic Castle Cake? It is sure to impress kids and adults alike.

Bake the batter in two 9 x 5-inch/23 x 13-cm loaf pans. Increase the recipe baking time by approximately 10 minutes. Let cool before frosting. Dye the frosting yellow. Trim all the sides of each cake until they are level and the cakes are rectangular. For the main section of the castle, place one cake on a platter or foil-covered cardboard. Cut the remaining cake in half vertically, and stand on the end of each side of the main section. Attach each end cake piece using about 1 tablespoon of yellow frosting and a wooden skewer. Frost the entire castle with yellow frosting. Place approximately one quarter of the frosting in a piping bag fitted with a small star tip. Pipe the frosting decoratively around the outer edges of the cake. Pipe a line of frosting around the entire cake where the cakes are joined.

Decorate with jelly fruits or gumdrops as shown on page 45. Press the cookie into one side of the castle to form the gate. Attach 3 short pieces of licorice to the door with a little frosting.

Dye two thirds of the decorating marzipan red. Form spires out of the red marzipan and place on the castle roof. Dye a small amount of the marzipan orange and form 2 pennant flags. Attach each flag to one end of a toothpick and stick the toothpicks in the cake on either side of the gate. Dye the remainder of the marzipan green and form a long cord. Flatten the cord with a fork and place along the bottom edge of the castle to form the grass.

Candy Basket

1 quantity Chocolate Cake
(see page 8)

1 quantity Buttercream
Frosting—white (see page 18)

yellow food coloring

gumdrops

chocolate drops

licorice rolls

junior mints

Baking the batter in a kugelhopf pan adds the texture needed to create a basket-like appearance. Be sure to spread the buttercream so that the raised parts of the form are only slightly covered with frosting. Then fill the cake with any candy you desire.

Bake the cake in a 10-inch/25-cm kugelhopf pan. Let cool completely before frosting.

Color the frosting with the yellow food coloring to the desired shade. Spread a thin layer of frosting around the cake. Then add more frosting, keeping it thin over the raised areas of the cake and filling in the indentations with more frosting.

Fill the hole with candy to your liking, making sure to fill it to the brim so some candy spills from the cake when it is sliced.

All-Day Lollipop Cake

1 quantity Banana Cake
(see page 10)

1 quantity Whipped Sour Cream
Frosting (see page 21)

assortment of lollipops

1 package jelly fruits or gumdrops
in assorted colors

This is the perfect cake to surprise any child. And best of all, it only takes minutes to decorate. Perfect if you forgot that special someone's birthday.

Bake the cake in a 10 x 12-inch/25 x 30-cm rectangular cake pan. Let cool completely before frosting.

When cooled, frost the cake evenly all around. Use a palette knife to create a very even surface on top. You can chill the cake at this stage if necessary. Do not refrigerate the cake with the candy decorations in place as they will draw the moisture and soften.

Place the jelly candies around the edge of the cake. Insert the lollipops into the surface. Serve immediately.

Marshmallow Cake

1 quantity Chocolate Cake
(see page 8)

1 quantity Dark Chocolate
Frosting
(see page 19)

12–15 two-toned marshmallows

Marshmallows always go down a charm with kids, and taste even better when they're on a delicious chocolate cake. You can easily substitute pink and white mini-marshmallows for the two-toned marshmallows.

Bake the batter in two 9-inch/23-cm round cake pans. Let cool completely before frosting.

When cool, frost the top of one of the cakes. Place the second cake on top and use the remaining frosting to cover the cake evenly. Use a palette knife to create an even surface on top of the cake.

Cut the marshmallows into thin slices and distribute evenly over the surface of the cake.

Flower Petal Cake

1 quantity Yogurt Sponge Cake (see page 16)

1 quantity Buttercream Frosting—white (see page 18)

malted milk balls, or other small chocolate candy

1 quantity Dark Chocolate Frosting (see page 19)

jelly fruits in assorted colors

yellow shoelace licorice or candy string

gummi discs

There is lots of room for variation with this design. Vary the candies or color the white frosting for a different effect—it will always taste delicious.

Bake the cake in a 10-inch/25-cm round cake pan. Let cool completely before frosting.

Cut out the middle area of the cake using a 3- or 4-inch/7.5- or 10-cm round cookie cutter, glass, or bowl. Press down hard and remove the center portion of the cake. Cut the remaining outer circle of cake into wedges.

Frost the wedges with the Buttercream Frosting. Decorate each wedge with a malted milk ball. Frost the center of the cake with the Dark Chocolate Frosting. Line the outer edge of the cake with jelly fruits. Create the center of the blossom with a candy string, a gummi disc, and jelly fruits, as shown on page 53. Place the cake on a platter and arrange the wedges around it, leaving some space between the cake and the wedges.

Tic-Tac-Toe Cake

1 quantity Chocolate Cake
(see page 8)

1 quantity Buttercream
Frosting—white (see page 18)

red shoelace licorice

black licorice pieces

It's every kid's favorite game, and this delicious version will have them asking to play another round!

Bake the cake in a 10 x 12-inch/25 x 30-cm rectangular cake pan. Let cool completely, then slice the cake in half horizontally.

Frost the top of one layer, place the other layer on top, and frost both together.

Lay 4 lengths of red shoelace licorice vertically and horizontally across the frosted cake to form 9 squares. Use whole shoelace licorice and licorice pieces to form Xs and Os.

Bunny Cake

1 quantity Carrot Cake
(see page 14)

1 quantity Cream Cheese Coconut
Frosting (see page 20)

2 cups grated coconut

pink food coloring

gummi discs

jelly fruits

red licorice string

Not just for birthdays, this cake would be lovely at Easter time as a special treat. Of course, you can color the coconut flakes any color you desire.

Bake the cake in a 10 x 12-inch/25 x 30-cm rectangular cake pan. Let cool. Using a 5-inch/13-cm round cookie cutter or glass, cut out 2 circles to form the head and body. Cut out 2 elliptical pieces to form the ears. Cut out 4 equal-sized triangles to form the paws.

Preheat the oven to 300°F/150°C. Frost all the pieces. Place the coconut in a bowl and carefully mix with the pink food coloring. Dry in an oven for 20 minutes. Stir occasionally so that the coconut does not brown. Let cool.

Sprinkle the frosted cake with the colored coconut. Arrange the pieces to form the rabbit, either directly on the serving platter or in a gift box. Use the gummi discs and jelly fruits to form the eyes. Use the licorice string for the whiskers and mouth. Use 2 more jelly fruits for the belly button and nose.

Irresistible Chocolate Spider Cake

1 quantity Chocolate Cake
(see page 8)

1 quantity Dark Chocolate
Frosting (see page 19)

½ cup white chocolate chips

1 scant tsp vegetable shortening

¼ quantity Decorating Marzipan
(see page 22)

unsweetened cocoa, for dusting

red licorice string

2 small red and white candies

This ghoulish cake makes a perfect Halloween party centerpiece or a great gift for anyone who loves something different!

Bake the batter in two 9-inch/23-cm round cake pans. Let cool completely before frosting.

Frost the top of one cake, place the other cake on top, and frost the whole cake . Before the frosting hardens, place the white chocolate chips and shortening in a small, zip-top plastic freezer bag. Place in a microwave oven and cook on High for 45 seconds. Squeeze gently and carefully. If necessary, cook for an additional 10–15 seconds; squeeze until the chips have melted. Make a small diagonal cut in a bottom corner of the bag; squeeze the mixture onto the cake to form a series of 4–5 concentric circles.

Using a knife or a toothpick, immediately draw 8–10 lines through the circles at regular intervals from the center to the edges of the cake to form the web.

Shape some marzipan into the spider's body, and dust generously with cocoa. Place in the center of the web. Use some red licorice string for legs and small red and white candies for eyes.

Cook's Tip: If you don't have a microwave oven, melt the chocolate chips in a small bowl over a pan of hot water. Place in the plastic bag and proceed with the recipe.

Floral Cupcakes

1 quantity Carrot Cake
(see page 14)

½ quantity Whipped Sour Cream
Frosting (see page 21)

2 quantities Decorating Marzipan
(see page 22)

red food coloring

green food coloring

The humble cupcake is transformed into something spectacular in this recipe. You can use any cake batter for this recipe, depending on your personal taste, although we recommend the Carrot Cake.

Bake the batter in 12 paper cupcake cups which have been placed in a standard 12-cup muffin pan. Reduce the baking time to approximately 30 minutes. Let the cupcakes cool in the pan for 10 minutes, then invert onto a cooling rack and cool completely. If any batter is left over, repeat the baking process with the remainder.

Frost the tops of the cupcakes.

Tint three quarters of the marzipan pink by kneading in some red food coloring. Roll out the marzipan between 2 pieces of plastic wrap or a cut-open plastic freezer bag. The thinner the marzipan, the more delicate the rosebuds. With a cookie cutter, cut out 48 small discs of marzipan. Set aside. Knead together the remaining red marzipan. Form twelve 1½-inch/3.75-cm "fingers," to make the center of the rosebud. Arrange 4 petals around the center, overlapping each petal to create a rose.

Color the remaining marzipan green. Mold small pieces that will form the beginning of the stem; they should become narrower toward one end. Press each rose onto a stem and place one flower on each cupcake.

Daisy Cake

1 quantity Sour Cream Pound Cake (see page 12)

1 quantity Buttercream Frosting—white (see page 18)

yellow and red food coloring

candy flowers

candy buttons

Perfect for any older girl on your birthday list, this cake is pretty without being too cute. The coloring is your choice; it is equally pretty in white, light blue, or pink.

Bake the batter in two 9-inch/23-cm round cake pans. Let cool completely before frosting.

Dye the frosting with the yellow food coloring. Add a few drops of red for a slightly more orange shade. When the cakes are sufficiently cooled, frost the top of one of them. Place the second cake on top of the first and use the remaining frosting to cover the cake evenly. Use a palette knife to create a slightly wavy surface.

Distribute the candy flowers on the top and sides of the cake and scatter the candy buttons over the surface. Complete with candles, if desired.

Adult Birthday Cakes

The following recipes provide lots of fun ideas for cakes for grown-ups, and are perfect to present as a gift or to bring to a party. The personal touch is always appreciated, so surprise someone on their big day with a stunning homemade creation.

Crazy Banana Cake

1 quantity Banana Cake
(see page 10)

1 quantity Dark Chocolate
Frosting (see page 19)

½ cup coconut flakes

banana-shaped candies

popcorn

This cake requires little preparation for the topping, and the unusual addition of the popcorn makes this especially fun to eat.

Bake the cake in a 9-inch/23-cm round cake pan. Let cool completely before frosting.

Slice the cake in half horizontally. Frost the top of the bottom layer and place the second layer on top. Frost the cake completely.

Sprinkle the sides of the cake with coconut flakes. Decorate the top of the cake with candy bananas and popcorn.

Heart with a Bow Cake

1 quantity Sour Cream Pound Cake (see page 12)

1 quantity Whipped Sour Cream Frosting (see page 21)

red food coloring

red and white dot candies

So simple, yet so romantic, this cake is perfect for the love-struck teen or a Valentine's Day party.

Bake the cake in a 13 x 12-inch/33 x 30-cm heart-shaped cake pan. Let cool.

Add a few drops of red food coloring to the frosting and mix. Keep mixing in the food coloring until you reach a shade of pink that you like.

Apply the frosting with a palette knife, forming an uneven, relief-like surface texture.

Apply the dot candies on the upper right-hand corner of the cake, forming a bow pattern.

Keep the cake covered and chilled until ready to serve.

Play Your Music Cake

1 quantity Yogurt Sponge Cake
(see page 16)

½ quantity Buttercream
Frosting—white (see page 18)

cornstarch, for dusting

1 lb 8 oz/700 g ready-to-use white
fondant

blue food coloring

*Bring yourself right up to date with this delicious personal music player cake, a great idea
for music fans.*

Bake the cake in a 10 x 12-inch/25 x 30-cm rectangular cake pan. Let cool completely
before frosting.

Cut the cake horizontally. Frost the top of one layer, place the second layer
on top, and thinly frost the remainder of the cake. Dust a counter with cornstarch.
Using a rolling pin lightly dusted with cornstarch, roll the fondant into a 14 x
16-inch/35 x 40-cm rectangle. Carefully lay the fondant over the frosted cake and
smooth onto the cake. Use a soft brush to dust off any cornstarch. Cut the extra
fondant overlapping the sides of the cake with a pizza wheel.

Knead half of the fondant again. Shape 2 long cords, and roll the remaining fondant
as directed above. Using cookie cutters or a small knife, cut out into thin strips, 5
triangles, and 1 circle.

Dye the remaining fondant light blue. Shape two earphones as depicted. Roll out
the remaining fondant and cut into a 4 x 6-inch/10 x 15-cm rectangle and a circle 5
inches/13 cm in diameter. Place on the cake as shown on page 71, then decorate with
the triangles, strips, and circle as depicted. Lay the earphone cords on the cake and
attach the earplugs. If you have any fondant left over, you can make musical notes,
the birthday boy or girl's name, or his or her favorite song title, and place this on the
blue screen.

Golfer's Cake

1 quantity Chocolate Cake
(see page 8)

1 quantity Dark Chocolate
Frosting (see page 19)

1 cup coconut flakes

green food coloring

10–12 oz/280–345 g ready-to-use
fondant

orange food coloring

licorice string

1 wooden skewer

For the golfer in your life, this whimsical cake is sure to impress.

Bake the cake in a 10 x 12-inch/25 x 30-cm sheet cake pan. Let cool completely before frosting.

Slice the cake in half horizontally. Frost the top of the bottom layer and place the second layer on top. Frost the cake completely. On the lower left-hand corner of the cake, scoop out a hole for the golf ball. Frost the inside of the hole.

Preheat the oven to 300°F/150°C. Place the coconut in a bowl and carefully mix with the green food coloring. Dry in the oven for 20 minutes. Stir occasionally so that the coconut does not brown. Sprinkle the coconut over the cake to form grass, avoiding the hole.

Roll two golf balls out of the fondant. Using a coarse grater, create the indentations characteristic of a golf ball. Place one ball in the hole. Dye the remaining fondant and form a tee. Insert a small wooden skewer into the tee so it can withstand the weight of the golf ball. Wrap the licorice string around the tee and set the tee into the cake, securing it in the hole with the wooden skewer. Set the golf ball on top. Thinly roll out the fondant and, using a cookie cutter, stamp out the age of the birthday boy or girl, then place it on the cake. You can also use Decorating Marzipan (see page 22) for the numbers.

Gardener's Cake

1 quantity Chocolate Cake
(see page 8)

1 quantity Dark Chocolate
Frosting (see page 19)

1 cup coconut flakes

green food coloring

brown food coloring

mini-mints

candy flowers

¼ quantity Decorating Marzipan
(see page 22)

brown food coloring

Surprise any amateur gardener with this delightful cake, and reap smiles all round.

Bake the cake in a 10 x 12-inch/25 x 30-cm sheet cake pan. Let cool completely before frosting. Slice off the edges of the cake all around. Place the cut portions in a food processor with the blade attachment and process until small crumbs form. Set on a tray and let dry until needed.

Slice the cake in half horizontally. Frost the top of the bottom layer and place the second layer on top. Frost the cake completely.

Preheat the oven to 300°F/150°C. Place the coconut in a bowl and carefully mix with the green food coloring. Dry in the oven for 20 minutes. Stir occasionally so that the coconut does not brown.

Place a wide strip of paper or cardboard on the frosted cake. Sprinkle the coconut over the frosted cake. Remove the cardboard and sprinkle the dark crumbs into the gap to create the "soil." Place the mints along the border of the soil. Decorate the coconut grass with candy flowers.

Color the marzipan with the brown food coloring and use to make a garden fork and trowel. Place these on one corner of the cake.

Football Field Cake

2 quantities Yogurt Sponge Cake
(see page 16)

1 lemon

1 quantity Buttercream Frosting
(see page 18)

3 sheets gelatin

¾ cup clear apple juice

green food coloring

6 oz/175 g white chocolate

Score a touchdown with this great cake. It would be perfect for any aspiring quarterback in your family.

Bake the cake in a 13 x 18-inch/33 x 36-cm sheet cake pan. Let cool completely before frosting.

Slice the cake in half horizontally. Finely grate the lemon peel and fold under the frosting. Coat one layer of the cake with a quarter of the frosting. Place the second layer on top and completely frost the cake. Refrigerate.

Soak the gelatin in cold water for 10 minutes. Bring the apple juice to a boil and remove from the heat. Squeeze any water from the gelatin and dissolve in the hot liquid, then stir in green food coloring to achieve the desired shade of green. Let cool. Once the liquid has cooled but has not begun to gel, carefully cover the surface of the cake. Refrigerate again, until the gelatin has gelled completely, approximately 3 hours.

Chop the white chocolate and melt in bowl over a double boiler. Put into a piping bag fitted with a fine tip and carefully pipe the yard lines and playing field outlines onto the cake.

To make the goals, melt the remaining white chocolate as directed above. Place a sheet of parchment paper on a counter, and thinly and evenly distribute the chocolate on the paper. Just before the chocolate hardens, use a small knife to cut out the outlines of the goals and carefully remove the chocolate from around the goals. Insert the goals into the cake.

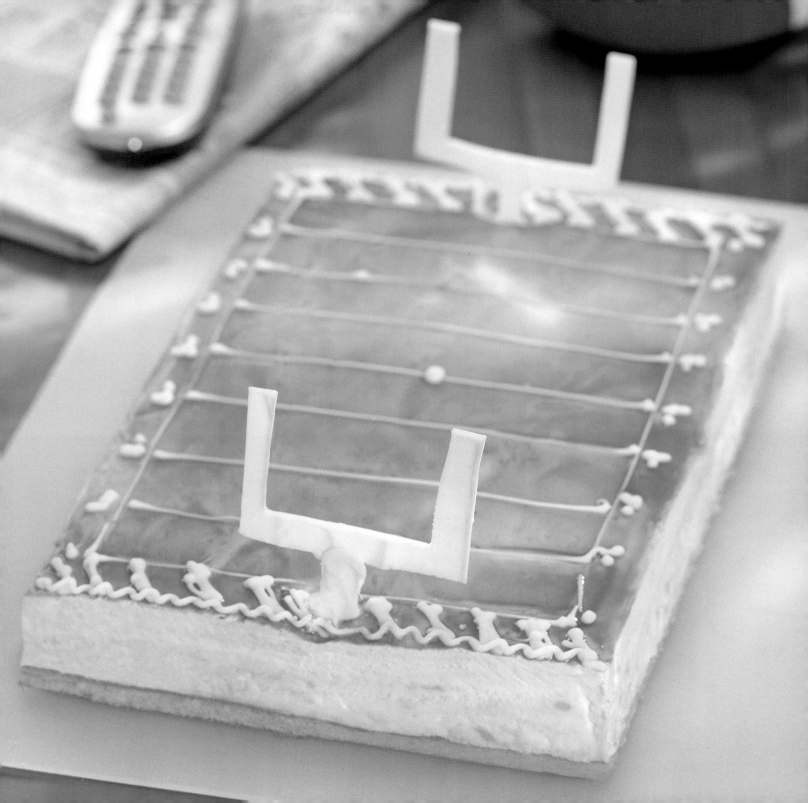

Baseball Cap Cake

1 quantity Yogurt Sponge Cake (see page 16)

1 quantity Buttercream Frosting—white (see page 18)

green food coloring

1 orange gumdrop

green licorice candy string

brown licorice candy string

Score a game-winning home run with this fanciful cap-shaped cake. Any baseball fan will love you for it.

Bake the cake in an 8¼-inch/21-cm ball-shaped cake pan (these are available commercially, or you can use an ovenproof flat-bottomed stainless steel bowl). Let cool completely before frosting.

Place the cake on a counter with the flat side down. Using a very sharp long knife, slice a piece about 1 inch/2.5 cm high off the bottom of the cake. Cut this lower section in half (discard the second half or use for another purpose).

Align the half-circle along the edge of the round cake on a large tray, trimming to shape the inside of the cake to fit around the sphere, like the bill of the cap.

Color the frosting with the food coloring and frost the cap and bill.

Place a gumdrop to represent the button. Use the green licorice string to make the seam in the cap. Use more string to shape the number on the bill. Wrap the brown licorice string along the base of the cake.

Using licorice string, write in the team number or better yet, his or her age.

Flower Frame Cake

1 quantity Chocolate Cake
(see page 8)

1 quantity Buttercream
Frosting—white (see page 18)

black licorice, to frame

orange and green candy string, to
form the flower

sugar drop candies in 5 assorted
colors, or chocolate lentil mints

1 red gummi disc

Say it with flowers—in a whole new way—with this delicious and pretty cake.

Bake the cake in a 9-inch/23-cm square cake pan. Let cool completely before frosting.

Slice the cake in half horizontally. Frost the top of the bottom layer and place the second layer on top. Frost the cake completely.

Lay the licorice around the edge of the cake, cutting it to fit if necessary. Cut the orange candy string into pieces approximately 8 inches/20 cm in length. Then outline the petals of a flower on the cake as shown on page 81. Use a long piece of green candy string to shape the stem. Cut two 2-inch/5-cm pieces of the green string, placing them halfway along the stem to form small leaves. If desired, add 2 very short pieces of string to form the bud. Fill in the petals of the flower and the 2 stem leaves. Place the gummi disc in the middle of the blossom.

High Heel Cake

2 quantities Sour Cream Pound Cake (see page 12)

1 quantity Buttercream Frosting—white (see page 18)

pink food coloring

4 quantities Decorating Marzipan (see page 22)

red food coloring

brown food coloring

One for the ladies, this is the perfect novelty cake for anyone with a serious shoe habit!

Bake the batter in a 9-inch/23-cm round cake pan and an 8-inch/20-cm round cake pan. Let cool completely before frosting.

Slice each cake in half. Color the frosting light pink. Frost the top side of the bottom layer of each cake. Place the top layer of each cake on top of the bottom layer. Lightly frost the surface and sides of each cake.

Color 2 quantities of the marzipan pink. Roll out the pink marzipan, and cover the cakes. Place one cake on top of the other.

Color 1 quantity of the marzipan red and use it to form a shoe. Place the shoe on top of the top cake.

Color two thirds of the final quantity of marzipan brown, leaving the remainder uncolored. Roll out the brown marzipan and, using a small cookie cutter, cut out small discs. Place the discs on the cake. Form the uncolored marzipan into little dots and distribute them evenly over the shoe.

Berry Cake

2 quantities Chocolate Cake
(see page 8)

1 lb 4 oz/550 g semisweet
chocolate pieces

6 tbsp vegetable shortening

6 oz/175 g white chocolate drops

8 fl oz/225 ml heavy cream

few drops vanilla extract

3 tbsp confectioners' sugar

1 pint/450 ml raspberries

Create a special cake in record time. This European-style birthday cake looks classy but is actually very easy to make.

Bake the batter in a 9-inch/23-cm round cake pan and an 8-inch/20-cm round cake pan. Let cool completely before frosting.

Place the larger cake on a cooling rack. Place the smaller cake on top of the larger one.

Melt the chocolate and vegetable shortening in a double boiler, or put the chocolate pieces in a metal bowl placed over a pan of simmering water. The chocolate will melt slowly, so leave it alone (no need to stir) and watch it carefully. Stir to blend the chocolate and shortening, keeping the glaze warm in the double boiler.

Pour the glaze over the cake. Decorate the surface of the cake with the white chocolate drops and let cool.

Carefully transfer the cake to a serving platter, using a large palette knife to support the entire weight of the cake.

Shortly before serving, whip the cream to soft peaks, gradually adding the vanilla extract and sugar. Spoon the whipped cream on top of the cake. If necessary, rinse the raspberries in cold water and let drain. Scatter the raspberries over the surface of the cake, and serve immediately.

Billiards Cake

1 quantity Yogurt Sponge Cake
(see page 16)

1 quantity Buttercream
Frosting—white (see page 18)

3 quantities Decorating Marzipan
(see page 22)

green food coloring

brown food coloring

red food coloring

Rack 'em up! This cake will have your pool buddies lined up for seconds.

Bake the cake in a 10 x 12-inch/25 x 30-cm sheet cake pan. Let cool completely before frosting.

Slice the cake in half horizontally. Frost the top of the bottom layer and place the second layer on top. Frost the cake completely.

Color 1 quantity of marzipan green. Roll out and cover the cake as directed in the basic directions.

Color 1 quantity of marzipan brown and shape three quarters of it into the billiards cue. Shape the remaining brown marzipan into 6 strands of equal length. Place these in the corners and on the sides of the cake as depicted.

Halve the remaining marzipan. Dye one half red and shape into billiard balls. Shape the remaining uncolored marzipan into 6 strands slightly longer than the brown strands. Place these behind the brown strand as shown on page 87. Roll out the remaining uncolored marzipan as directed, then cut into a thin strip. Wrap the marzipan strip around the thick end of the billiard cue. Place the cue on the cake.

Rose Blossom Cake

2 quantities Yogurt Sponge Cake
(see page 16)

1 quantity Buttercream
Frosting—white (see page 18)

pink food coloring

1 lb 4 oz/560 g ready-to-use
fondant

crystallized rose petals

Classic and elegant, you cannot fail to impress with this pretty pink creation.

Bake the batter in a 6-inch/14-cm round cake pan and an 8-inch/20-cm round cake pan. Let cool completely before frosting.

Slice each cake in half. Color the frosting light pink. Frost the top of the bottom layer of each cake. Place the top layer of each cake on top of the bottom layer. Lightly frost the surface and sides of each cake.

Dye the fondant pink. Roll out and cover the cakes. Place one cake on top of the other.

Decorate the cakes with the crystallized rose petals.

Lace Cake

1 quantity Chocolate Cake
(see page 8)

1 quantity Dark Chocolate
Frosting (see page 19)

about ¼ cup cocoa powder, for
dusting

about ¼ cup confectioners' sugar,
for dusting

1 x 8-inch/20-cm round doily or
plastic stencil

chocolate-covered coffee beans

silver candy nonpareils

As easy as it is delicious, this is a smart way to decorate a cake quickly and in style. If you are really in a hurry, just trim the cake and sprinkle with cocoa and sugar without frosting it first.

Bake the cake in a 9-inch/23-cm round cake pan. Cool completely before frosting.

Slice the cake in half and frost the top of the bottom layer. Place the second layer on top and frost the top and sides of the cake.

Just before serving, fill a small fine-mesh strainer with cocoa. Dust the cake by gently tapping as you move the strainer over the cake.

Place the doily on the cake, fill the strainer with sugar and dust the cake.

Carefully remove the doily—the lace pattern will show up on the cake. Decorate with coffee beans and nonpareils.

Bottle of Wine Cake

1 quantity Chocolate Cake
(see page 8)

2 quantities Decorating Marzipan
(see page 22)

green food coloring

yellow food coloring

red food coloring

This cake makes a great gift and a stunning display piece.

Bake the cake in a 10 x 12-inch/25 x 30-cm sheet cake pan. When fully cooled, cut the cake into a bottle shape using a sharp knife.

Color two thirds of the marzipan green, divide the remainder in half, and dye it orange and red. Roll out the green and orange marzipan and cover the cake with the green marzipan. Using a cookie cutter, cut out the age of the birthday guest from the orange marzipan. Cut the marzipan into a strip to create the bottle label. Place the label in the center of the cake and tuck under the cake.

Gather up the remaining green and orange marzipan and, together with the red marzipan, mold them into a cork. Place the cork beside the bottle.

Strawberry Cake

1 quantity Sour Cream Pound Cake (see page 12)

2 quantities Whipped Sour Cream Frosting (see page 21)

1 quantity Decorating Marzipan (see page 22)

green food coloring

A little trick turns a heart-shaped cake into this fruity birthday treat. Just add a little strawberry syrup to the frosting for a delicious twist.

Bake the cake in a 12 x 13-inch/30 x 35-cm heart-shaped cake pan. Let cool as directed.

Add red food coloring to the frosting and mix, creating a dark red. Keep mixing in food coloring until you reach a shade of pink you like. Cut the cake in half horizontally. Frost the bottom layer and replace the top. Cover the cake with the remaining frosting. Using the tines of a fork, score the surface to create the "seeds" of the strawberry.

Dye the marzipan two shades of green and roll out thinly as directed in the basic instructions. Using a pizza wheel, cut the marzipan into leaves and arrange them decoratively at the top of the strawberry, thereby transforming the heart shape into a strawberry shape.

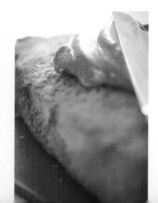

Index